The Congo and Other Poems

VACHEL LINDSAY

DOVER PUBLICATIONS, INC.
New York

Note

The American poet Vachel Lindsay (born in Springfield, Illinois, 1879; died there, 1931) is remembered today chiefly for his efforts to revive the oral tradition in poetry. He described two of his most popular poems, "The Congo" and "The Santa-Fe Trail," as "experiments in which I endeavor to carry [a] vaudeville form back towards the old Greek precedent of the half-chanted lyric." His most important work, *The Congo and Other Poems*, was first published in 1914, to great popular acclaim, establishing him, along with Edgar Lee Masters and Carl Sandburg, as part of the Chicago "Renaissance." This volume contained, in addition to those works "intended to be read aloud, or chanted," the antiwar poem "Abraham Lincoln Walks at Midnight" and the series of "Moon Poems."

In the present edition, which is based on the 1915 edition, the original anomalies in punctuation and orthography have for the most part been left unaltered. However, some changes have been made to the organization of sections in order to establish consistency throughout the volume.

DOVER THRIFT EDITIONS

General Editor: Stanley Appelbaum

Editor of This Volume: Shane Weller

Published in Canada by General Publishing Company, Ltd., 30 Lesmill Road, Don Mills, Toronto, Ontario.
Published in the United Kingdom by Constable and Company, Ltd., 3 The Lanchesters, 162–164 Fulham Palace Road, London W6 9ER.

This Dover edition, first published in 1992, is a republication of the 1915 edition of the work originally published by The Macmillan Company, New York, in 1914. The original Introduction by Harriet Monroe is not included in the Dover edition, for which the Note and alphabetical lists were specially prepared.

Manufactured in the United States of America
Dover Publications, Inc., 31 East 2nd Street, Mineola, N.Y. 11501

Library of Congress Cataloging-in-Publication Data

Lindsay, Vachel, 1879–1931.
    The Congo and other poems / Vachel Lindsay.
        p.   cm. — (Dover thrift editions)
    "Republication of the work originally published by the Macmillan Company, New York, in 1914"—T.p. verso.
    ISBN 0-486-27272-9 (pbk.)
    I. Title. II. Series.
PS3523.I58C6   1992
811'.52—dc20

                                                        92-11702
                                                           CIP

Contents

First Section: Poems Intended to Be Read Aloud, or Chanted

Second Section: Incense

Third Section

First Section: A Miscellany Called "The Christmas Tree"

Second Section: Rhymes for Gloriana

Fourth Section: Twenty [*sic*] Poems in Which the Moon Is the Principal Figure of Speech

Fifth Section: War. September 1, 1914: Intended to Be Read Aloud

FIRST SECTION

POEMS INTENDED TO BE READ ALOUD, OR CHANTED

The Congo

A Study of the Negro Race

I. THEIR BASIC SAVAGERY

Fat black bucks in a wine-barrel room,
Barrel-house kings, with feet unstable,
Sagged and reeled and pounded on the table,

A deep rolling bass.

Pounded on the table,
Beat an empty barrel with the handle of a broom,
Hard as they were able,
Boom, boom, BOOM,
With a silk umbrella and the handle of a broom,
Boomlay, boomlay, boomlay, BOOM.
THEN I had religion, THEN I had a vision.
I could not turn from their revel in derision.
THEN I SAW THE CONGO, CREEPING THROUGH THE BLACK,

More deliberate. Solemnly chanted.

CUTTING THROUGH THE FOREST WITH A GOLDEN TRACK.
Then along that riverbank
A thousand miles
Tattooed cannibals danced in files;
Then I heard the boom of the blood-lust song
And a thigh-bone beating on a tin-pan gong.

A rapidly piling climax of speed and racket.

And "BLOOD" screamed the whistles and the fifes of the warriors,
"BLOOD" screamed the skull-faced, lean witch-doctors,
"Whirl ye the deadly voo-doo rattle,
Harry the uplands,
Steal all the cattle,
Rattle-rattle, rattle-rattle,
Bing.
Boomlay, boomlay, boomlay, BOOM,"
A roaring, epic, rag-time tune

With a philosophic pause.

From the mouth of the Congo
To the Mountains of the Moon.

3

Death is an Elephant,
Torch-eyed and horrible,
Foam-flanked and terrible.
BOOM, steal the pygmies,
BOOM, kill the Arabs,
BOOM, kill the white men,
HOO, HOO, HOO.

*Shrilly and
with a heavily
accented metre.*

Listen to the yell of Leopold's ghost
Burning in Hell for his hand-maimed host.
Hear how the demons chuckle and yell
Cutting his hands off, down in Hell.
Listen to the creepy proclamation,
Blown through the lairs of the forest-nation,
Blown past the white-ants' hill of clay,
Blown past the marsh where the butterflies play:—

*Like the wind
in the chimney.*

"Be careful what you do,
Or Mumbo-Jumbo, God of the Congo,
And all of the other
Gods of the Congo,
Mumbo-Jumbo will hoo-doo you,
Mumbo-Jumbo will hoo-doo you,
Mumbo-Jumbo will hoo-doo you."

*All the o
sounds very
golden. Heavy
accents very
heavy. Light
accents very
light. Last line
whispered.*

II. THEIR IRREPRESSIBLE HIGH SPIRITS

Wild crap-shooters with a whoop and a call
Danced the juba in their gambling-hall
And laughed fit to kill, and shook the town,
And guyed the policemen and laughed them down
With a boomlay, boomlay, boomlay, BOOM.

*Rather shrill
and high.*

THEN I SAW THE CONGO, CREEPING THROUGH THE
   BLACK,
CUTTING THROUGH THE FOREST WITH A GOLDEN
   TRACK.

*Read exactly as
in first section.*

A negro fairyland swung into view,
A minstrel river
Where dreams come true.
The ebony palace soared on high
Through the blossoming trees to the evening sky.
The inlaid porches and casements shone
With gold and ivory and elephant-bone.
And the black crowd laughed till their sides were
   sore

*Lay emphasis
on the delicate
ideas. Keep as
light-footed as
possible.*

At the baboon butler in the agate door,
And the well-known tunes of the parrot band
That trilled on the bushes of that magic land.

A troupe of skull-faced witch-men came   *With*
Through the agate doorway in suits of flame,   *pomposity.*
Yea, long-tailed coats with a gold-leaf crust
And hats that were covered with diamond-dust.
And the crowd in the court gave a whoop and a call
And danced the juba from wall to wall.
But the witch-men suddenly stilled the throng   *With a great*
With a stern cold glare, and a stern old song:—   *deliberation*
"Mumbo-Jumbo will hoo-doo you." . . .   *and ghostliness.*
Just then from the doorway, as fat as shotes,   *With*
Came the cake-walk princes in their long red coats,   *overwhelming*
Canes with a brilliant lacquer shine,   *assurance, good*
And tall silk hats that were red as wine.   *cheer, and pomp.*
And they pranced with their butterfly partners   *With growing*
      there,   *speed and*
Coal-black maidens with pearls in their hair,   *sharply marked*
Knee-skirts trimmed with the jassamine sweet,   *dance-rhythm.*
And bells on their ankles and little black feet.
And the couples railed at the chant and the frown
Of the witch-men lean, and laughed them down.
(O rare was the revel, and well worth while
That made those glowering witch-men smile.)

The cake-walk royalty then began
To walk for a cake that was tall as a man
To the tune of "Boomlay, boomlay, BOOM,"
While the witch-men laughed, with a sinister air,   *With a touch of*
And sang with the scalawags prancing there:—   *negro dialect,*
"Walk with care, walk with care,   *and as rapidly*
Or Mumbo-Jumbo, God of the Congo,   *as possible*
And all of the other   *toward the end.*
Gods of the Congo,
Mumbo-Jumbo will hoo-doo you.
Beware, beware, walk with care,
Boomlay, boomlay, boomlay, boom.
Boomlay, boomlay, boomlay, boom,
Boomlay, boomlay, boomlay, boom,
Boomlay, boomlay, boomlay,
BOOM."

Oh rare was the revel, and well worth while
That made those glowering witch-men smile.

Slow philosophic calm.

III. THE HOPE OF THEIR RELIGION

A good old negro in the slums of the town
Preached at a sister for her velvet gown.
Howled at a brother for his low-down ways,
His prowling, guzzling, sneak-thief days.
Beat on the Bible till he wore it out
Starting the jubilee revival shout.
And some had visions, as they stood on chairs,
And sang of Jacob, and the golden stairs,
And they all repented, a thousand strong
From their stupor and savagery and sin and wrong
And slammed with their hymn books till they
    shook the room
With "glory, glory, glory,"
And "Boom, boom, BOOM."

Heavy bass. With a literal imitation of camp-meeting racket, and trance.

THEN I SAW THE CONGO, CREEPING THROUGH THE
    BLACK
CUTTING THROUGH THE JUNGLE WITH A GOLDEN
    TRACK.
And the gray sky opened like a new-rent veil
And showed the apostles with their coats of mail.
In bright white steele they were seated round
And their fire-eyes watched where the Congo
    wound.
And the twelve Apostles, from their thrones on
    high

Exactly as in the first section. Begin with terror and power, end with joy.

Thrilled all the forest with their heavenly cry:—
"Mumbo-Jumbo will die in the jungle;
Never again will he hoo-doo you,
Never again will he hoo-doo you."

Sung to the tune of "Hark, ten thousand harps and voices."

Then along that river, a thousand miles
The vine-snared trees fell down in files.
Pioneer angels cleared the way
For a Congo paradise, for babes at play,
For sacred capitals, for temples clean.
Gone were the skull-faced witch-men lean.

With growing deliberation and joy.

There, where the wild ghost-gods had wailed
A million boats of the angels sailed
With oars of silver, and prows of blue
And silken pennants that the sun shone through.
'Twas a land transfigured, 'twas a new creation.
Oh, a singing wind swept the negro nation
And on through the backwoods clearing flew:—
"Mumbo-Jumbo is dead in the jungle.
Never again will he hoo-doo you.
Never again will he hoo-doo you."

In a rather high key—as delicately as possible.

To the tune of "Hark, ten thousand harps and voices."

Redeemed were the forests, the beasts and the men,
And only the vulture dared again
By the far, lone Mountains of the Moon
To cry, in the silence, the Congo tune:—
"Mumbo-Jumbo will hoo-doo you,
Mumbo-Jumbo will hoo-doo you.
Mumbo . . . Jumbo . . . will . . . hoo-doo . . .
    you."

Dying down into a penetrating, terrified whisper.

The Santa-Fe Trail

(A Humoresque)

I asked the old Negro, "What is that bird that sings so well?" He answered: "That is the Rachel-Jane." "Hasn't it another name, lark, or thrush, or the like?" "No. Jus' Rachel-Jane."

I. IN WHICH A RACING AUTO COMES FROM THE EAST

This is the order of the music of the morning:—
First, from the far East comes but a crooning.
The crooning turns to a sunrise singing.
Hark to the *calm*-horn, *balm*-horn, *psalm*-horn.
Hark to the *faint*-horn, *quaint*-horn, *saint*-
    horn. . . .

To be sung delicately, to an improvised tune.

Hark to the *pace*-horn, *chase*-horn, *race*-horn.
And the holy veil of the dawn has gone.
Swiftly the brazen car comes on.

To be sung or read with great speed.

It burns in the East as the sunrise burns.
I see great flashes where the far trail turns.
Its eyes are lamps like the eyes of dragons.
It drinks gasoline from big red flagons.
Butting through the delicate mists of the morning,
It comes like lightning, goes past roaring.
It will hail all the wind-mills, taunting, ringing,
Dodge the cyclones,
Count the milestones,
On through the ranges the prairie-dog tills—
Scooting past the cattle on the thousand hills. . . .
Ho for the tear-horn, scare-horn, dare-horn,
Ho for the *gay*-horn, *bark*-horn, *bay*-horn.
Ho for Kansas, land that restores us
When houses choke us, and great books bore us!
Sunrise Kansas, harvester's Kansas,
A million men have found you before us.

To be read or sung in a rolling bass, with some deliberation.

II. In Which Many Autos Pass Westward

I want live things in their pride to remain.
I will not kill one grasshopper vain
Though he eats a hole in my shirt like a door.
I let him out, give him one chance more.
Perhaps, while he gnaws my hat in his whim,
Grasshopper lyrics occur to him.

In an even, deliberate, narrative manner.

I am a tramp by the long trail's border,
Given to squalor, rags and disorder.
I nap and amble and yawn and look,
Write fool-thoughts in my grubby book,
Recite to the children, explore at my ease,
Work when I work, beg when I please,
Give crank-drawings, that make folks stare
To the half-grown boys in the sunset glare,
And get me a place to sleep in the hay
At the end of a live-and-let-live day.

I find in the stubble of the new-cut weeds
A whisper and a feasting, all one needs:
The whisper of the strawberries, white and red
Here where the new-cut weeds lie dead.

But I would not walk all alone till I die
Without some life-drunk horns going by.
Up round this apple-earth they come
Blasting the whispers of the morning dumb:—
Cars in a plain realistic row.
And fair dreams fade
When the raw horns blow.

On each snapping pennant
A big black name:—
The careering city
Whence each car came.
They tour from Memphis, Atlanta, Savannah,   *Like a train-*
Tallahassee and Texarkana.   *caller in a*
They tour from St. Louis, Columbus, Manistee, *Union Depot.*
They tour from Peoria, Davenport, Kankakee.
Cars from Concord, Niagara, Boston,
Cars from Topeka, Emporia, and Austin.
Cars from Chicago, Hannibal, Cairo.
Cars from Alton, Oswego, Toledo.
Cars from Buffalo, Kokomo, Delphi,
Cars from Lodi, Carmi, Loami.
Ho for Kansas, land that restores us
When houses choke us, and great books bore us!
While I watch the highroad
And look at the sky,
While I watch the clouds in amazing grandeur
Roll their legions without rain
Over the blistering Kansas plain—
While I sit by the milestone
And watch the sky,
The United States
Goes by.

Listen to the iron-horns, ripping, racking.   *To be given very*
Listen to the quack-horns, slack and clacking.   *harshly, with a*
Way down the road, trilling like a toad,   *snapping*
Here comes the *dice*-horn, here comes the *vice*- *explosiveness.*
    horn,
Here comes the *snarl*-horn, *brawl*-horn, *lewd*-horn,
Followed by the *prude*-horn, bleak and squeak-
    ing:—

(Some of them from Kansas, some of them from
      Kansas.)
Here comes the *hod*-horn, *plod*-horn, *sod*-horn,
Nevermore-to-*roam*-horn, *loam*-horn, *home*-horn.
(Some of them from Kansas, some of them from
      Kansas.)

Far away the Rachel-Jane   *To be read or*
Not defeated by the horns   *sung, well-nigh*
Sings amid a hedge of thorns:—   *in a whisper.*
"Love and life,
Eternal youth—
Sweet, sweet, sweet, sweet,
Dew and glory,
Love and truth,
Sweet, sweet, sweet, sweet."

WHILE SMOKE-BLACK FREIGHTS ON THE DOUBLE-   *Louder and*
      TRACKED RAILROAD,   *louder, faster*
DRIVEN AS THOUGH BY THE FOUL-FIEND'S OX-   *and faster.*
      GOAD,
SCREAMING TO THE WEST COAST, SCREAMING TO
      THE EAST,
CARRY OFF A HARVEST, BRING BACK A FEAST,
HARVESTING MACHINERY AND HARNESS FOR THE
      BEAST.
THE HAND-CARS WHIZ, AND RATTLE ON THE RAILS,
THE SUNLIGHT FLASHES ON THE TIN DINNER-PAILS.
And then, in an instant,   *In a rolling*
Ye modern men,   *bass, with*
Behold the procession once again,   *increasing*
     deliberation.
Listen to the iron-horns, ripping, racking,   *With a*
Listen to the *wise*-horn, desperate-to-*advise*-horn,   *snapping*
Listen to the *fast*-horn, *kill*-horn, *blast*-horn. . . .   *explosiveness.*

Far away the Rachel-Jane   *To be sung or*
Not defeated by the horns   *read well-nigh*
Sings amid a hedge of thorns:—   *in a whisper.*
Love and life,
Eternal youth,
Sweet, sweet, sweet, sweet,
Dew and glory,
Love and truth.
Sweet, sweet, sweet, sweet.

The mufflers open on a score of cars
With wonderful thunder,
CRACK, CRACK, CRACK,
CRACK-CRACK, CRACK-CRACK,
CRACK-CRACK-CRACK, . . .
Listen to the gold-horn . . .
Old-horn . . .
Cold-horn . . .

To be brawled in the beginning with a snapping explosiveness, ending in a languorous chant.

And all of the tunes, till the night comes down
On hay-stack, and ant-hill, and wind-bitten town.
Then far in the west, as in the beginning,
Dim in the distance, sweet in retreating,
Hark to the faint-horn, quaint-horn, saint-horn,
Hark to the calm-horn, balm-horn, psalm-
    horn. . . .

To be sung to exactly the same whispered tune as the first five lines.

They are hunting the goals that they understand:—
San-Francisco and the brown sea-sand.
My goal is the mystery the beggars win.
I am caught in the web the night-winds spin.
The edge of the wheat-ridge speaks to me.
I talk with the leaves of the mulberry tree.
And now I hear, as I sit all alone
In the dusk, by another big Santa-Fe stone,
The souls of the tall corn gathering round
And the gay little souls of the grass in the ground.
Listen to the tale the cotton-wood tells.
Listen to the wind-mills, singing o'er the wells.
Listen to the whistling flutes without price
Of myriad prophets out of paradise.
Harken to the wonder
That the night-air carries. . . .
Listen . . . to . . . the . . . whisper . . .
Of . . . the . . . prairie . . . fairies

This section beginning sonorously, ending in a languorous whisper.

    Singing o'er the fairy plain:—
    "Sweet, sweet, sweet, sweet.
    Love and glory,
    Stars and rain,
    Sweet, sweet, sweet, sweet. . . ."

To the same whispered tune as the Rachel-Jane song—but very slowly.

The Firemen's Ball

SECTION ONE

"Give the engines room,
Give the engines room."
Louder, faster
The little band-master
Whips up the fluting,
Hurries up the tooting.
He thinks that he stands,
The reins in his hands,
In the fire-chief's place
In the night alarm chase.
The cymbals whang,
The kettledrums bang:—
"Clear the street,
Clear the street,
Clear the street—Boom, boom.
In the evening gloom,
In the evening gloom,
Give the engines room,
Give the engines room,
Lest souls be trapped
In a terrible tomb."
The sparks and the pine-brands
Whirl on high
From the black and reeking alleys
To the wide red sky.
Hear the hot glass crashing,
Hear the stone steps hissing.
Coal black streams
Down the gutters pour.
There are cries for help
From a far fifth floor.
For a longer ladder
Hear the fire-chief call.
Listen to the music
Of the firemen's ball.
Listen to the music

*To be read, or
chanted, with
the heavy
buzzing bass of
fire-engines
pumping.*

*In this passage
the reading or
chanting is
shriller and
higher.*

Of the firemen's ball.
" 'Tis the
NIGHT
Of doom,"
Say the ding-dong doom-bells.
"NIGHT
Of doom,"
Say the ding-dong doom-bells.
Faster, faster
The red flames come.
"Hum grum," say the engines,
"Hum grum grum."
"Buzz, buzz,"
Says the crowd.
"See, see,"
Calls the crowd.
"Look out,"
Yelps the crowd
And the high walls fall:—
Listen to the music
Of the firemen's ball.
Listen to the music
Of the firemen's ball.
" 'Tis the
NIGHT
Of doom,"
Say the ding-dong doom-bells.
NIGHT
Of doom,
Say the ding-dong doom-bells.
Whangaranga, whangaranga,
Whang, whang, whang,
Clang, clang, clangaranga,
Clang, clang, clang.
Clang—a—ranga—
Clang—a—ranga—
Clang,
Clang,
Clang.
Listen—to—the—music—
Of the firemen's ball—

*To be read or
chanted in a
heavy bass.*

*Shriller and
higher.*

Heavy bass.

*Bass, much
slower.*

SECTION TWO

"Many's the heart that's breaking
If we could read them all
After the ball is over." (An old song.)

Scornfully, gaily
The bandmaster sways,
Changing the strain
That the wild band plays.
With a red and royal intoxication,
A tangle of sounds
And a syncopation,
Sweeping and bending
From side to side,
Master of dreams,
With a peacock pride.
A lord of the delicate flowers of delight
He drives compunction
Back through the night.
Dreams he's a soldier
Plumed and spurred,
And valiant lads
Arise at his word,
Flaying the sober
Thoughts he hates,
Driving them back
From the dream-town gates.
How can the languorous
Dancers know
The red dreams come
When the good dreams go?
" 'Tis the
NIGHT
Of love,"
Call the silver joy-bells,
"NIGHT
Of love,"
Call the silver joy-bells.
Honey and wine,
Honey and wine.

*To be read or
sung slowly
and softly, in
the manner of
lustful,
insinuating
music.*

*To be read or
chanted slowly
and softly in
the manner of
lustful
insinuating
music.*

Sing low, now, violins,
Sing, sing low,
Blow gently, wood-wind,
Mellow and slow.
Like midnight poppies
The sweethearts bloom.
Their eyes flash power,
Their lips are dumb.
Faster and faster
Their pulses come,
Though softer now
The drum-beats fall.
Honey and wine,
Honey and wine.
'Tis the firemen's ball,
'Tis the firemen's ball.

"I am slain,"
Cries true-love
There in the shadow.
"And I die,"
Cries true-love,
There laid low.
"When the fire-dreams come,
The wise dreams go."
BUT HIS CRY IS DROWNED
BY THE PROUD BAND-MASTER.
And now great gongs whang,
Sharper, faster,
And kettledrums rattle
And hide the shame
With a swish and a swirk
In dead love's name.
Red and crimson
And scarlet and rose
Magical poppies
The sweethearts bloom.
The scarlet stays
When the rose-flush goes,
And love lies low
In a marble tomb.

*With a climax
of whispered
mourning.*

*Suddenly
interrupting.
To be read or
sung in a heavy
bass. First eight
lines as harsh
as possible.
Then gradually
musical and
sonorous.*

" 'Tis the
NIGHT
Of doom,"
Call the ding-dong doom-bells.
"NIGHT
Of Doom,"
Call the ding-dong doom-bells.

      Hark how the piccolos still make cheer.   *Sharply*
      "'Tis a moonlight night in the spring of   *interrupting in*
           the year."   *a very high key.*
CLANGARANGA, CLANGARANGA,   *Heavy bass.*
CLANG . . . CLANG . . . CLANG.
CLANG . . . A . . . RANGA . . .
CLANG . . . A . . . RANGA . . .
CLANG . . . CLANG . . . CLANG . . .
LISTEN . . . TO . . . THE . . . MUSIC . . .
OF . . . THE . . . FIREMEN'S BALL . . .
LISTEN . . . TO . . . THE . . . MUSIC . . .
OF . . . THE . . . FIREMEN'S . . . BALL . . .

SECTION THREE

In Which, contrary to Artistic Custom, the moral of the piece is placed before the reader.

(From the first Khandaka of the Mahavagga: "There Buddha thus addressed his disciples: 'Everything, O mendicants, is burning. With what fire is it burning? I declare unto you it is burning with the fire of passion, with the fire of anger, with the fire of ignorance. It is burning with the anxieties of birth, decay and death, grief, lamentation, suffering and despair. . . . A disciple, . . . becoming weary of all that, divests himself of passion. By absence of passion, he is made free.' ")

I once knew a teacher,   *To be intoned*
Who turned from desire,   *after the*
Who said to the young men   *manner of a*
"Wine is a fire."   *priestly service.*
Who said to the merchants:—
"Gold is a flame
That sears and tortures
If you play at the game."
I once knew a teacher

Who turned from desire
Who said to the soldiers,
"Hate is a fire."
Who said to the statesmen:—
"Power is a flame
That flays and blisters
If you play at the game."
I once knew a teacher
Who turned from desire,
Who said to the lordly,

"Pride is a fire."
Who thus warned the revellers:—
"Life is a flame.
Be cold as the dew
Would you win at the game
With hearts like the stars,
With hearts like the stars."
SO BEWARE,
SO BEWARE,
SO BEWARE OF THE FIRE.
Clear the streets,
BOOM, BOOM,
Clear the streets,
BOOM, BOOM,
GIVE THE ENGINES ROOM,
GIVE THE ENGINES ROOM,
LEST SOULS BE TRAPPED
IN A TERRIBLE TOMB.
SAYS THE SWIFT WHITE HORSE
TO THE SWIFT BLACK HORSE:—
"THERE GOES THE ALARM,
THERE GOES THE ALARM.
THEY ARE HITCHED, THEY ARE OFF,
THEY ARE GONE IN A FLASH,
AND THEY STRAIN AT THE DRIVER'S IRON
    ARM."
CLANG . . . A . . . RANGA . . . CLANG . . .
    A . . . RANGA . . .
CLANG . . . CLANG . . . CLANG. . . .
CLANG . . . A . . . RANGA . . . CLANG . . .
    A . . . RANGA . . .

*Interrupting
very loudly for
the last time.*

CLANG . . . CLANG . . . CLANG. . . .
CLANG . . . A . . . RANGA . . . CLANG . . .
    A . . . RANGA . . .
CLANG . . . CLANG . . . CLANG. . . .

The Master of the Dance

A chant to which it is intended a group of children shall dance and improvise pantomime led by their dancing-teacher.

I

A master deep-eyed
Ere his manhood was ripe,
He sang like a thrush,
He could play any pipe.
So dull in the school
That he scarcely could spell,
He read but a bit,
And he figured not well.
A bare-footed fool,
Shod only with grace;
Long hair streaming down
Round a wind-hardened face;
He smiled like a girl,
Or like clear winter skies,
A virginal light
Making stars of his eyes.
In swiftness and poise,
A proud child of the deer,
A white fawn he was,
Yet a fawn without fear.
No youth thought him vain,
Or made mock of his hair,
Or laughed when his ways
Were most curiously fair.
A mastiff at fight,
He could strike to the earth
The envious one
Who would challenge his worth.

However we bowed
To the schoolmaster mild,
Our spirits went out
To the fawn-footed child.
His beckoning led
Our troop to the brush.
We found nothing there
But a wind and a hush.
He sat by a stone
And he looked on the ground,
As if in the weeds
There was something profound.
His pipe seemed to neigh,
Then to bleat like a sheep,
Then sound like a stream
Or a waterfall deep.
It whispered strange tales,
Human words it spoke not.
Told fair things to come,
And our marvellous lot
If now with fawn-steps
Unshod we advanced
To the midst of the grove
And in reverence danced.
We obeyed as he piped
Soft grass to young feet,
Was a medicine mighty,
A remedy meet.
Our thin blood awoke,
It grew dizzy and wild,
Though scarcely a word
Moved the lips of a child.
Our dance gave allegiance,
It set us apart,
We tripped a strange measure,
Uplifted of heart.

II

We thought to be proud
Of our fawn everywhere.
We could hardly see how

Simple books were a care.
No rule of the school
This strange student could tame.
He was banished one day,
While we quivered with shame.
He piped back our love
On a moon-silvered night,
Enticed us once more
To the place of delight.
A greeting he sang
And it made our blood beat,
It tramped upon custom
And mocked at defeat.
He builded a fire
And we tripped in a ring,
The embers our books
And the fawn our good king.
And now we approached
All the mysteries rare
That shadowed his eyelids
And blew through his hair.
That spell now was peace
The deep strength of the trees,
The children of nature
We clambered her knees.
Our breath and our moods
Were in tune with her own,
Tremendous her presence,
Eternal her throne.
The ostracized child
Our white foreheads kissed,
Our bodies and souls
Became lighter than mist.
Sweet dresses like snow
Our small lady-loves wore,
Like moonlight the thoughts
That our bosoms upbore.
Like a lily the touch
Of each cold little hand.
The loves of the stars
We could now understand.

O quivering air!
O the crystalline night!
O pauses of awe
And the faces swan-white!
O ferns in the dusk!
O forest-shrined hour!
O earth that sent upward
The thrill and the power,
To lift us like leaves,
A delirious whirl,
The masterful boy
And the delicate girl!
What child that strange night-time
Can ever forget?
His fealty due
And his infinite debt
To the folly divine,
To the exquisite rule
Of the perilous master,
The fawn-footed fool?

III

Now soldiers we seem,
And night brings a new thing,
A terrible ire,
As of thunder awing.
A warrior power,
That old chivalry stirred,
When knights took up arms,
As the maidens gave word.
THE END OF OUR WAR,
WILL BE GLORY UNTOLD,
WHEN THE TOWN LIKE A GREAT
BUDDING ROSE SHALL UNFOLD!
Near, nearer that war,
And that ecstasy comes,
We hear the trees beating
Invisible drums.
The fields of the night
Are starlit above,

Our girls are white torches
Of conquest and love.
No nerve without will,
And no breast without breath,
We whirl with the planets
That never know death!

The Mysterious Cat

A chant for a children's pantomime dance, suggested by a picture painted by George Mather Richards.

I saw a proud, mysterious cat,
I saw a proud, mysterious cat
Too proud to catch a mouse or rat—
Mew, mew, mew.

But catnip she would eat, and purr,
But catnip she would eat, and purr.
And goldfish she did much prefer—
Mew, mew, mew.

I saw a cat—'twas but a dream,
I saw a cat—'twas but a dream
Who scorned the slave that brought her cream—
Mew, mew, mew.

Unless the slave were dressed in style,
Unless the slave were dressed in style
And knelt before her all the while—
Mew, mew, mew.

Did you ever hear of a thing like that?
Did you ever hear of a thing like that?
Did you ever hear of a thing like that?
Oh, what a proud mysterious cat.
Oh, what a proud mysterious cat.
Oh, what a proud mysterious cat.
Mew . . . mew . . . mew.

A Dirge for a Righteous Kitten

To be intoned, all but the two italicized lines, which are to be spoken in a snappy, matter-of-fact way.

Ding-dong, ding-dong, ding-dong.
Here lies a kitten good, who kept
A kitten's proper place.
He stole no pantry eatables,
Nor scratched the baby's face.
He let the alley-cats alone.
He had no yowling vice.
His shirt was always laundried well,
He freed the house of mice.
Until his death he had not caused
His little mistress tears,
He wore his ribbon prettily,
He washed behind his ears.
Ding-dong, ding-dong, ding-dong.

Yankee Doodle

This poem is intended as a description of a sort of Blashfield mural painting on the sky. To be sung to the tune of Yankee Doodle, yet in a slower, more orotund fashion. It is presumably an exercise for an entertainment on the evening of Washington's Birthday.

Dawn this morning burned all red
Watching them in wonder.
There I saw our spangled flag
Divide the clouds asunder.
Then there followed Washington.
Ah, he rode from glory,
Cold and mighty as his name
And stern as Freedom's story.
Unsubdued by burning dawn

Led his continentals.
Vast they were, and strange to see
In gray old regimentals:—
Marching still with bleeding feet,
Bleeding feet and jesting—
Marching from the judgment throne
With energy unresting.
How their merry quickstep played—
Silver, sharp, sonorous,
Piercing through with prophecy
The demons' rumbling chorus—
Behold the ancient powers of sin
And slavery before them!—
Sworn to stop the glorious dawn,
The pit-black clouds hung o'er them.
Plagues that rose to blast the day
Fiend and tiger faces,
Monsters plotting bloodshed for
The patient toiling races.
Round the dawn their cannon raged,
Hurling bolts of thunder,
Yet before our spangled flag
Their host was cut asunder.
Like a mist they fled away. . . .
Ended wrath and roaring.
Still our restless soldier-host
From East to West went pouring.

High beside the sun of noon
They bore our banner splendid.
All its days of stain and shame
And heaviness were ended.
Men were swelling now the throng
From great and lowly station—
Valiant citizens to-day
Of every tribe and nation.
Not till night their rear-guard came,
Down the west went marching,
And left behind the sunset-rays
In beauty overarching.
War-god banners lead us still,

Rob, enslave and harry
Let us rather choose to-day
The flag the angels carry—
Flag we love, but brighter far—
Soul of it made splendid:
Let its days of stain and shame
And heaviness be ended.
Let its fifes fill all the sky,
Redeemed souls marching after,
Hills and mountains shake with song,
While seas roll on in laughter.

The Black Hawk War of the Artists

WRITTEN FOR LORADO TAFT'S STATUE OF
BLACK HAWK AT OREGON, ILLINOIS

To be given in the manner of the Indian Oration and the Indian
War-Cry.

Hawk of the Rocks,
Yours is our cause to-day.
Watching your foes
Here in our war array,
Young men we stand,
Wolves of the West at bay.
    Power, power for war
    Comes from these trees divine;
    Power from the boughs,
    Boughs where the dew-beads shine,
    Power from the cones—
    Yea, from the breath of the pine!

Power to restore
All that the white hand mars.
See the dead east
Crushed with the iron cars—
Chimneys black
Blinding the sun and stars!

Hawk of the pines,
Hawk of the plain-winds fleet,
You shall be king
There in the iron street,
Factory and forge
Trodden beneath your feet.

There will proud trees
Grow as they grow by streams.
There will proud thoughts
Walk as in warrior dreams.
There will proud deeds
Bloom as when battle gleams!

Warriors of Art,
We will hold council there,
Hewing in stone
Things to the trapper fair,
Painting the gray
Veils that the spring moons wear,
This our revenge,
This one tremendous change:
Making new towns,
Lit with a star-fire strange,
Wild as the dawn
Gilding the bison-range.

All the young men
Chanting your cause that day,
Red-men, new-made
Out of the Saxon clay,
Strong and redeemed,
Bold in your war-array!

The Jingo and the Minstrel

AN ARGUMENT FOR THE MAINTENANCE OF PEACE AND
GOODWILL WITH THE JAPANESE PEOPLE

Glossary for the uninstructed and the hasty: Jimmu Tenno,
ancestor of all the Japanese Emperors; Nikko, Japan's loveliest
shrine; Iyeyasu, her greatest statesman; Bushido, her code of
knighthood; The Forty-seven Ronins, her classic heroes; Nogi, her
latest hero; Fuji, her most beautiful mountain.

"Now do you know of Avalon   *The minstrel*
    That sailors call Japan?   *speaks.*
She holds as rare a chivalry
    As ever bled for man.
King Arthur sleeps at Nikko hill
    Where Iyeyasu lies,
And there the broad Pendragon flag
    In deathless splendor flies."

"*Nay, minstrel, but the great ships come*   *The jingo*
    From out the sunset sea.   *answers.*
We cannot greet the souls they bring
    With welcome high and free.
How can the Nippon nondescripts
    That weird and dreadful band
Be aught but what we find them here—
    The blasters of the land?"

"First race, first men from anywhere   *The minstrel*
    To face you, eye to eye.   *replies.*
For *that* do you curse Avalon
    And raise a hue and cry?
These toilers cannot kiss your hand,
    Or fawn with hearts bowed down.
Be glad for them, and Avalon,
    And Arthur's ghostly crown.

"No doubt your guests, with sage debate
    In grave things gentlemen
Will let your trade and farms alone

And turn them back again.
But why should brawling braggarts rise
    With hasty words of shame
To drive them back like dogs and swine
    Who in due honor came?"

"We cannot give them honor, sir.   The jingo
    We give them scorn for scorn.   answers.
And Rumor steals around the world
    All white-skinned men to warn
Against this sleek silk-merchant here
    And viler coolie-man
And wrath within the courts of war
    Brews on against Japan!"

"Must Avalon, with hope forlorn,   The minstrel
    Her back against the wall,   replies.
Have lived her brilliant life in vain
    While ruder tribes take all?
Must Arthur stand with Asian Celts,
    A ghost with spear and crown,
Behind the great Pendragon flag
    And be again cut down?

"Tho Europe's self shall move against
    High Jimmu Tenno's throne
The Forty-seven Ronin Men
    Will not be found alone.
For Percival and Bedivere
    And Nogi side by side
Will stand,—with mourning Merlin there,
    Tho all go down in pride.

"But has the world the envious dream—
    Ah, such things cannot be,—
To tear their fairy-land like silk
    And toss it in the sea?
Must venom rob the future day
    The ultimate world-man
Of rare Bushido, code of codes,
    The fair heart of Japan?

"Go, be the guest of Avalon.
    Believe me, it lies there

Behind the mighty gray sea-wall
　　Where heathen bend in prayer:
Where peasants lift adoring eyes
　　To Fuji's crown of snow.
King Arthur's knights will be your hosts,
　　So cleanse your heart, and go.

"And you will find but gardens sweet
　　Prepared beyond the seas,
And you will find but gentlefolk
　　Beneath the cherry-trees.
So walk you worthy of your Christ
　　Tho church bells do not sound,
And weave the bands of brotherhood
　　On Jimmu Tenno's ground."

I Heard Immanuel Singing

(The poem shows the Master, with his work done, singing to free
his heart in Heaven.)

This poem is intended to be half said, half sung, very softly, to
the well-known tune:—

"Last night I lay a-sleeping,
There came a dream so fair,
I stood in Old Jerusalem
Beside the temple there,—" etc.

Yet this tune is not to be fitted on, arbitrarily. It is here given to
suggest the manner of handling rather than determine it.

I heard Immanuel singing   *To be sung.*
Within his own good lands,
I saw him bend above his harp.
I watched his wandering hands
Lost amid the harp-strings;
Sweet, sweet I heard him play.
His wounds were altogether healed.
Old things had passed away.

All things were new, but music.
The blood of David ran
Within the Son of David,
Our God, the Son of Man.
He was ruddy like a shepherd.
His bold young face, how fair.
Apollo of the silver bow
Had not such flowing hair.

I saw Immanuel singing
On a tree-girdled hill.
The glad remembering branches
Dimly echoed still
The grand new song proclaiming
The Lamb that had been slain.
New-built, the Holy City
Gleamed in the murmuring plain.

*To be read very
softly, but in
spirited
response.*

The crowning hours were over.
The pageants all were past.
Within the many mansions
The hosts, grown still at last,
In homes of holy mystery
Slept long by crooning springs
Or waked to peaceful glory,
A universe of Kings.

He left his people happy.
He wandered free to sigh
Alone in lowly friendship
With the green grass and the sky.
He murmured ancient music
His red heart burned to sing
Because his perfect conquest
Had grown a weary thing.

To be sung.

No chant of gilded triumph—
His lonely song was made
Of Art's deliberate freedom;
Of minor chords arrayed
In soft and shadowy colors
That once were radiant flowers:—

The Rose of Sharon, bleeding
In Olive-shadowed bowers:—

And all the other roses
In the songs of East and West
Of love and war and worshipping,
And every shield and crest
Of thistle or of lotus
Or sacred lily wrought
In creeds and psalms and palaces
And temples of white thought:—

All these he sang, half-smiling   *To be read very*
And weeping as he smiled,   *softly, yet in*
Laughing, talking to his harp   *spirited*
As to a new-born child:—   *response.*
As though the arts forgotten
But bloomed to prophecy
These careless, fearless harp-strings,
New-crying in the sky.
"When this his hour of sorrow   *To be sung.*
For flowers and Arts of men
Has passed in ghostly music,"
I asked my wild heart then—
What will he sing to-morrow,
What wonder, all his own
Alone, set free, rejoicing,
With a green hill for his throne?
What will he sing to-morrow
What wonder all his own
Alone, set free, rejoicing,
With a green hill for his throne?

SECOND SECTION

INCENSE

An Argument

I. The Voice of the Man Impatient with Visions and Utopias

We find your soft Utopias as white
As new-cut bread, and dull as life in cells,
O, scribes who dare forget how wild we are
How human breasts adore alarum bells.
You house us in a hive of prigs and saints
Communal, frugal, clean and chaste by law.
I'd rather brood in bloody Elsinore
Or be Lear's fool, straw-crowned amid the straw.
Promise us all our share in Agincourt
Say that our clerks shall venture scorns and death,
That future ant-hills will not be too good
For Henry Fifth, or Hotspur, or Macbeth.
Promise that through to-morrow's spirit-war
Man's deathless soul will hack and hew its way,
Each flaunting Caesar climbing to his fate
Scorning the utmost steps of yesterday.
Never a shallow jester any more!
Let not Jack Falstaff spill the ale in vain.
Let Touchstone set the fashions for the wise
And Ariel wreak his fancies through the rain.

II. The Rhymer's Reply. Incense and Splendor

Incense and Splendor haunt me as I go.
Though my good works have been, alas, too few,
Though I do naught, High Heaven comes down to me,
And future ages pass in tall review.
I see the years to come as armies vast,
Stalking tremendous through the fields of time.
Man is unborn. To-morrow he is born,
Flame-like to hover o'er the moil and grime,
Striving, aspiring till the shame is gone,

35

Sowing a million flowers, where now we mourn—
Laying new, precious pavements with a song,
Founding new shrines, the good streets to adorn.
I have seen lovers by those new-built walls
Clothed like the dawn in orange, gold and red.
Eyes flashing forth the glory-light of love
Under the wreaths that crowned each royal head.
Life was made greater by their sweetheart prayers.
Passion was turned to civic strength that day—
Piling the marbles, making fairer domes
With zeal that else had burned bright youth away.
I have seen priestesses of life go by
Gliding in samite through the incense-sea—
Innocent children marching with them there,
Singing in flowered robes, "THE EARTH IS FREE":
While on the fair, deep-carved unfinished towers
Sentinels watched in armor, night and day—
Guarding the brazier-fires of hope and dream—
Wild was their peace, and dawn-bright their array!

A Rhyme about an Electrical Advertising Sign

I look on the specious electrical light
Blatant, mechanical, crawling and white,
Wickedly red or malignantly green
Like the beads of a young Senegambian queen.
Showing, while millions of souls hurry on,
The virtues of collars, from sunset till dawn,
By dart or by tumble of whirl within whirl,
Starting new fads for the shame-weary girl,
By maggoty motions in sickening line
Proclaiming a hat or a soup or a wine,
While there far above the steep cliffs of the street
The stars sing a message elusive and sweet.

Now man cannot rest in his pleasure and toil
His clumsy contraptions of coil upon coil
Till the thing he invents, in its use and its range,

Leads on to the marvellous CHANGE BEYOND CHANGE.
Some day this old Broadway shall climb to the skies,
As a ribbon of cloud on a soul-wind shall rise.
And we shall be lifted, rejoicing by night,
Till we join with the planets who choir their delight.
The signs in the street and the signs in the skies
Shall make a new Zodiac, guiding the wise,
And Broadway make one with that marvellous stair
That is climbed by the rainbow-clad spirits of prayer.

In Memory of a Child

The angels guide him now,
And watch his curly head,
And lead him in their games,
The little boy we led.

He cannot come to harm,
He knows more than we know,
His light is brighter far
Than daytime here below.

His path leads on and on,
Through pleasant lawns and flowers,
His brown eyes open wide
At grass more green than ours.

With playmates like himself,
The shining boy will sing,
Exploring wondrous woods,
Sweet with eternal spring.

Galahad, Knight Who Perished

A Poem Dedicated to All Crusaders against
the International and Interstate Traffic
in Young Girls

Galahad . . . soldier that perished . . . ages ago,
Our hearts are breaking with shame, our tears overflow.
Galahad . . . knight who perished . . . awaken again,
Teach us to fight for immaculate ways among men.
Soldiers fantastic, we pray to the star of the sea,
We pray to the mother of God that the bound may be free.
Rose-crowned lady from heaven, give us thy grace,
Help us the intricate, desperate battle to face
Till the leer of the trader is seen nevermore in the land,
Till we bring every maid of the age to one sheltering hand.
Ah, they are priceless, the pale and the ivory and red!
Breathless we gaze on the curls of each glorious head!
Arm them with strength mediaeval, thy marvellous dower,
Blast now their tempters, shelter their steps with thy power.
Leave not life's fairest to perish—strangers to thee,
Let not the weakest be shipwrecked, oh, star of the sea!

The Leaden-Eyed

Let not young souls be smothered out before
They do quaint deeds and fully flaunt their pride.
It is the world's one crime its babes grow dull,
Its poor are ox-like, limp and leaden-eyed.
Not that they starve, but starve so dreamlessly,
Not that they sow, but that they seldom reap,
Not that they serve, but have no gods to serve,
Not that they die, but that they die like sheep.

An Indian Summer Day on the Prairie

(IN THE BEGINNING)

The sun is a huntress young,
The sun is a red, red joy,
The sun is an Indian girl,
Of the tribe of the Illinois.

(MID-MORNING)

The sun is a smouldering fire,
That creeps through the high gray plain,
And leaves not a bush of cloud
To blossom with flowers of rain.

(NOON)

The sun is a wounded deer,
That treads pale grass in the skies,
Shaking his golden horns,
Flashing his baleful eyes.

(SUNSET)

The sun is an eagle old,
There in the windless west.
Atop of the spirit-cliffs
He builds him a crimson nest.

The Hearth Eternal

There dwelt a widow learned and devout,
Behind our hamlet on the eastern hill.
Three sons she had, who went to find the world.
They promised to return, but wandered still.
The cities used them well, they won their way,
Rich gifts they sent, to still their mother's sighs.

Worn out with honors, and apart from her,
They died as many a self-made exile dies.
The mother had a hearth that would not quench,
The deathless embers fought the creeping gloom.
She said to us who came with wondering eyes—
"This is a magic fire, a magic room."
The pine burned out, but still the coals glowed on,
Her grave grew old beneath the pear-tree shade,
And yet her crumbling home enshrined the light.
The neighbors peering in were half afraid.
Then sturdy beggars, needing fagots, came,
One at a time, and stole the walls, and floor.
They left a naked stone, but how it blazed!
And in the thunderstorm it flared the more.
And now it was that men were heard to say,
"This light should be beloved by all the town."
At last they made the slope a place of prayer,
Where marvellous thoughts from God came sweeping down.
They left their churches crumbling in the sun,
They met on that soft hill, one brotherhood;
One strength and valor only, one delight,
One laughing, brooding genius, great and good.
Now many gray-haired prodigals come home,
The place out-flames the cities of the land,
And twice-born Brahmans reach us from afar,
With subtle eyes prepared to understand.
Higher and higher burns the eastern steep,
Showing the roads that march from every place,
A steady beacon o'er the weary leagues,
At dead of night it lights the traveller's face!
Thus has the widow conquered half the earth,
She who increased in faith, though all alone,
Who kept her empty house a magic place,
Has made the town a holy angel's throne.

The Soul of the City Receives the Gift of the Holy Spirit

A Broadside Distributed in
Springfield, Illinois

Censers are swinging
Over the town;
Censers are swinging,
Look overhead!
Censers are swinging,
Heaven comes down.
City, dead city,
Awake from the dead!

Censers, tremendous,
Gleam overhead.
Wind-harps are ringing,
Wind-harps unseen—
Calling and calling:—
"Wake from the dead.
Rise, little city,
Shine like a queen."

Soldiers of Christ
For battle grow keen.
Heaven-sent winds
Haunt alley and lane.
Singing of life
In town-meadows green
After the toil
And battle and pain.

Incense is pouring
Like the spring rain
Down on the mob
That moil through the street.
Blessed are they
Who behold it and gain
Power made more mighty
Thro' every defeat.

Builders, toil on.
Make all complete.
Make Springfield wonderful.
Make her renown
Worthy this day,
Till, at God's feet,
Tranced, saved forever,
Waits the white town.

Censers are swinging
Over the town,
Censers gigantic!
Look overhead!
Hear the winds singing:—
"Heaven comes down.
City, dead city,
Awake from the dead."

By the Spring, at Sunset

Sometimes we remember kisses,
Remember the dear heart-leap when they came:
Not always, but sometimes we remember
The kindness, the dumbness, the good flame
Of laughter and farewell.

                    Beside the road
Afar from those who said "Good-by" I write,
Far from my city task, my lawful load.

Sun in my face, wind beside my shoulder,
Streaming clouds, banners of new-born night
Enchant me now. The splendors growing bolder
Make bold my soul for some new wise delight.

I write the day's event, and quench my drouth,
Pausing beside the spring with happy mind.
And now I feel those kisses on my mouth,
Hers most of all, one little friend most kind.

I Went Down into the Desert

I went down into the desert
To meet Elijah—
Arisen from the dead.
I thought to find him in an echoing cave;
For so my dream had said.

I went down into the desert
To meet John the Baptist.
I walked with feet that bled,
Seeking that prophet lean and brown and bold.
I spied foul fiends instead.

I went down into the desert
To meet my God.
By him be comforted.
I went down into the desert
To meet my God.
And I met the devil in red.

I went down into the desert
To meet my God.
O, Lord my God, awaken from the dead!
I see you there, your thorn-crown on the ground,
I see you there, half-buried in the sand.
I see you there, your white bones glistening, bare,
The carrion-birds a-wheeling round your head.

Love and Law

True Love is founded in rocks of Remembrance
In stones of Forbearance and mortar of Pain.
The workman lays wearily granite on granite,
And bleeds for his castle 'mid sunshine and rain.

Love is not velvet, not all of it velvet,
Not all of it banners, not gold-leaf alone.

'Tis stern as the ages and old as Religion.
With Patience its watchword, and Law for its throne.

The Perfect Marriage

I

I hate this yoke; for the world's sake here put it on:
Knowing 'twill weigh as much on you till life is gone.
Knowing you love your freedom dear, as I love mine—
Knowing that love unchained has been our life's great wine:
Our one great wine (yet spent too soon, and serving none;
Of the two cups free love at last the deadly one).

II

We grant our meetings will be tame, not honey-sweet
No longer turning to the tryst with flying feet.
We know the toil that now must come will spoil the bloom
And tenderness of passion's touch, and in its room
Will come tame habit, deadly calm, sorrow and gloom.
Oh, how the battle scars the best who enter life!
Each soldier comes out blind or lame from the black strife.
Mad or diseased or damned of soul the best may come—
It matters not how merrily now rolls the drum,
The fife shrills high, the horn sings loud, till no steps lag—
And all adore that silken flame, Desire's great flag.

III

We will build strong our tiny fort, strong as we can—
Holding one inner room beyond the sword of man.
Love is too wide, it seems to-day, to hide it there.
It seems to flood the fields of corn, and gild the air—
It seems to breathe from every brook, from flowers to sigh—
It seems a cataract poured down from the great sky;
It seems a tenderness so vast no bush but shows
Its haunting and transfiguring light where wonder glows.
It wraps us in a silken snare by shadowy streams,
And wildering sweet and stung with joy your white soul
        seems

A flame, a flame, conquering day, conquering night,
Brought from our God, a holy thing, a mad delight.
But love, when all things beat it down, leaves the wide air,
The heavens are gray, and men turn wolves, lean with despair.
Ah, when we need love most, and weep, when all is dark,
Love is a pinch of ashes gray, with one live spark—
Yet on the hope to keep alive that treasure strange
Hangs all earth's struggle, strife and scorn, and desperate
      change.

IV

Love? . . . we will scarcely love our babes full many a time—
Knowing their souls and ours too well, and all our grime—
And there beside our holy hearth we'll hide our eyes—
Lest we should flash what seems disdain without disguise.
Yet there shall be no wavering there in that deep trial—
And no false fire or stranger hand or traitor vile—
We'll fight the gloom and fight the world with strong sword-
      play,
Entrenched within our block-house small, ever at bay—
As fellow-warriors, underpaid, wounded and wild,
True to their battered flag, their faith still undefiled!

Darling Daughter of Babylon

Too soon you wearied of our tears.
And then you danced with spangled feet,
Leading Belshazzar's chattering court
A-tinkling through the shadowy street.
With mead they came, with chants of shame.
DESIRE's red flag before them flew.
And Istar's music moved your mouth
And Baal's deep shames rewoke in you.

Now you could drive the royal car;
Forget our Nation's breaking load:
Now you could sleep on silver beds—
(Bitter and dark was our abode.)
And so, for many a night you laughed,

And knew not of my hopeless prayer,
Till God's own spirit whipped you forth
From Istar's shrine, from Istar's stair.

Darling daughter of Babylon—
Rose by the black Euphrates flood—
Again your beauty grew more dear
Than my slave's bread, than my heart's blood.
We sang of Zion, good to know,
Where righteousness and peace abide. . . .
What of your second sacrilege
Carousing at Belshazzar's side?

Once, by a stream, we clasped tired hands—
Your paint and henna washed away.
Your place, you said, was with the slaves
Who sewed the thick cloth, night and day.
You were a pale and holy maid
Toil-bound with us. One night you said:—
"Your God shall be my God until
I slumber with the patriarch dead."

Pardon, daughter of Babylon,
If, on this night remembering
Our lover walks under the walls
Of hanging gardens in the spring,
A venom comes from broken hope,
From memories of your comrade-song
Until I curse your painted eyes
And do your flower-mouth too much wrong.

The Amaranth

Ah, in the night, all music haunts me here. . . .
Is it for naught high Heaven cracks and yawns
And the tremendous Amaranth descends
Sweet with the glory of ten thousand dawns?

Does it not mean my God would have me say:—
"Whether you will or no, O city young,

The Traveller-Heart

*(To a Man Who Maintained That the Mausoleum Is the
Stateliest Possible Manner of Interment)*

I would be one with the dark, dark earth:—
Follow the plough with a yokel tread.
I would be part of the Indian corn,
Walking the rows with the plumes o'erhead.

I would be one with the lavish earth,
Eating the bee-stung apples red:
Walking where lambs walk on the hills;
By oak-grove paths to the pools be led.

I would be one with the dark-bright night
When sparkling skies and the lightning wed—
Walking on with the vicious wind
By roads whence even the dogs have fled.

I would be one with the sacred earth
On to the end, till I sleep with the dead.
Terror shall put no spears through me.
Peace shall jewel my shroud instead.

I shall be one with all pit-black things
Finding their lowering threat unsaid:
Stars for my pillow there in the gloom,—
Oak-roots arching about my head!

Stars, like daisies, shall rise through the earth,
Acorns fall round my breast that bled.
Children shall weave there a flowery chain,
Squirrels on acorn-hearts be fed:—

Fruit of the traveller-heart of me,
Fruit of my harvest-songs long sped:
Sweet with the life of my sunburned days
When the sheaves were ripe, and the apples red.

The North Star Whispers to the Blacksmith's Son

The North Star whispers: "You are one
Of those whose course no chance can change.
You blunder, but are not undone,
Your spirit-task is fixed and strange.

"When here you walk, a bloodless shade,
A singer all men else forget.
Your chants of hammer, forge and spade
Will move the prairie-village yet.

"That young, stiff-necked, reviling town
Beholds your fancies on her walls,
And paints them out or tears them down,
Or bars them from her feasting-halls.

"Yet shall the fragments still remain;
Yet shall remain some watch-tower strong
That ivy-vines will not disdain,
Haunted and trembling with your song.

"Your flambeau in the dusk shall burn,
Flame high in storms, flame white and clear;
Your ghost in gleaming robes return
And burn a deathless incense here."

THIRD SECTION

First Section: A Miscellany Called "The Christmas Tree"

This Section Is a Christmas Tree

This section is a Christmas tree:
Loaded with pretty toys for you.
Behold the blocks, the Noah's arks,
The popguns painted red and blue.
No solemn pine-cone forest-fruit,
But silver horns and candy sacks
And many little tinsel hearts
And cherubs pink, and jumping-jacks.
For every child a gift, I hope.
The doll upon the topmost bough
Is mine. But all the rest are yours.
And I will light the candles now.

The Sun Says His Prayers

"The sun says his prayers," said the fairy,
Or else he would wither and die.
"The sun says his prayers," said the fairy,
"For strength to climb up through the sky.
He leans on invisible angels,
And Faith is his prop and his rod.
The sky is his crystal cathedral.
And dawn is his altar to God."

Popcorn, Glass Balls, and Cranberries (As It Were)

THE LION

The Lion is a kingly beast.
He likes a Hindu for a feast.
And if no Hindu he can get,
The lion-family is upset.

He cuffs his wife and bites her ears
Till she is nearly moved to tears.
Then some explorer finds the den
And all is family peace again.

AN EXPLANATION OF THE GRASSHOPPER

The Grasshopper, the grasshopper,
I will explain to you:—
He is the Brownies' racehorse,
The fairies' Kangaroo.

THE DANGEROUS LITTLE BOY FAIRIES

In fairyland the little boys
Would rather fight than eat their meals.
They like to chase a gauze-winged fly
And catch and beat him till he squeals.
Sometimes they come to sleeping men
Armed with the deadly red-rose thorn,
And those that feel its fearful wound
Repent the day that they were born.

THE MOUSE THAT GNAWED THE OAK-TREE DOWN

The mouse that gnawed the oak-tree down
Began his task in early life.
He kept so busy with his teeth
He had no time to take a wife.

He gnawed and gnawed through sun and rain
When the ambitious fit was on,
Then rested in the sawdust till
A month of idleness had gone.

He did not move about to hunt
The coteries of mousie-men.
He was a snail-paced, stupid thing
Until he cared to gnaw again.

The mouse that gnawed the oak-tree down,
When that tough foe was at his feet—
Found in the stump no angel-cake
Nor buttered bread, nor cheese, nor meat—
The forest-roof let in the sky.
"This light is worth the work," said he.
"I'll make this ancient swamp more light,"
And started on another tree.

PARVENU

Where does Cinderella sleep?
By far-off day-dream river.
A secret place her burning Prince
Decks, while his heart-strings quiver.

Homesick for our cinder world,
Her low-born shoulders shiver;
She longs for sleep in cinders curled—
We, for the day-dream river

THE SPIDER AND THE GHOST OF THE FLY

Once I loved a spider
When I was born a fly,
A velvet-footed spider
With a gown of rainbow-dye.
She ate my wings and gloated.
She bound me with a hair.

She drove me to her parlor
Above her winding stair.
To educate young spiders
She took me all apart.

My ghost came back to haunt her.
I saw her eat my heart.

CRICKETS ON A STRIKE

The foolish queen of fairyland
From her milk-white throne in a lily-bell,
Gave command to her cricket-band
To play for her when the dew-drops fell.

But the cold dew spoiled their instruments
And they play for the foolish queen no more.
Instead those sturdy malcontents
Play sharps and flats in my kitchen floor.

How a Little Girl Danced

DEDICATED TO LUCY BATES

(*Being a reminiscence of certain private theatricals.*)

Oh, cabaret dancer, *I* know a dancer,
Whose eyes have not looked on the feasts that are vain.
I know a dancer, *I* know a dancer,
Whose soul has no bond with the beasts of the plain:
Judith the dancer, Judith the dancer,
With foot like the snow, and with step like the rain.

Oh, thrice-painted dancer, vaudeville dancer,
Sad in your spangles, with soul all astrain,
I know a dancer, *I* know a dancer,
Whose laughter and weeping are spiritual gain,
A pure-hearted, high-hearted maiden evangel,
With strength the dark cynical earth to disdain.

Flowers of bright Broadway, you of the chorus,
Who sing in the hope of forgetting your pain:
I turn to a sister of Sainted Cecilia,
A white bird escaping the earth's tangled skein:—
The music of God is her innermost brooding,
The whispering angels her footsteps sustain.

Oh, proud Russian dancer: praise for your dancing.
No clean human passion my rhyme would arraign.
You dance for Apollo with noble devotion,
A high cleansing revel to make the heart sane.
But Judith the dancer prays to a spirit
More white than Apollo and all of his train.

I know a dancer who finds the true Godhead,
Who bends o'er a brazier in Heaven's clear plain.
I know a dancer, I know a dancer,
Who lifts us toward peace, from this earth that is vain:
Judith the dancer, Judith the dancer,
With foot like the snow, and with step like the rain.

In Praise of Songs That Die

AFTER HAVING READ A GREAT DEAL
OF GOOD CURRENT POETRY IN THE
MAGAZINES AND NEWSPAPERS

Ah, they are passing, passing by,
Wonderful songs, but born to die!
Cries from the infinite human seas,
Waves thrice-winged with harmonies.
Here I stand on a pier in the foam
Seeing the songs to the beach go home,
Dying in sand while the tide flows back,
As it flowed of old in its fated track.
Oh, hurrying tide that will not hear
Your own foam-children dying near:
Is there no refuge-house of song,
No home, no haven where songs belong?
Oh, precious hymns that come and go!
You perish, and I love you so!

Factory Windows Are Always Broken

Factory windows are always broken.
Somebody's always throwing bricks,
Somebody's always heaving cinders,
Playing ugly Yahoo tricks.

Factory windows are always broken.
Other windows are let alone.
No one throws through the chapel-window
The bitter, snarling, derisive stone.

Factory windows are always broken.
Something or other is going wrong.
Something is rotten—I think, in Denmark.
End of the factory-window song. .

To Mary Pickford

MOVING-PICTURE ACTRESS

(On hearing she was leaving the moving-pictures
for the stage.)

Mary Pickford, doll divine,
Year by year, and every day
At the moving-picture play,
You have been my valentine.

Once a free-limbed page in hose,
Baby-Rosalind in flower,
Cloakless, shrinking, in that hour
How our reverent passion rose,
How our fine desire you won.
Kitchen-wench another day,
Shapeless, wooden every way.
Next, a fairy from the sun.

Once you walked a grown-up strand
Fish-wife siren, full of lure,
Snaring with devices sure
Lads who murdered on the sand.
But on most days just a child
Dimpled as no grown-folk are,
Cold of kiss as some north star,
Violet from the valleys wild.
Snared as innocence must be,
Fleeing, prisoned, chained, half-dead—
At the end of tortures dread
Roaring cowboys set you free.

Fly, O song, to her to-day,
Like a cowboy cross the land.
Snatch her from Belasco's hand
And that prison called Broadway.

All the village swains await
One dear lily-girl demure,
Saucy, dancing, cold and pure,
Elf who must return in state.

Blanche Sweet

Moving-Picture Actress

(After seeing the reel called "Oil and Water.")

Beauty has a throne-room
In our humorous town,
Spoiling its hob-goblins,
Laughing shadows down.
Rank musicians torture
Ragtime ballads vile,
But we walk serenely
Down the odorous aisle.
We forgive the squalor
And the boom and squeal
For the Great Queen flashes
From the moving reel.

Just a prim blonde stranger
In her early day,
Hiding brilliant weapons,
Too averse to play,
Then she burst upon us
Dancing through the night.
Oh, her maiden radiance,
Veils and roses white.
With new powers, yet cautious,
Not too smart or skilled,
That first flash of dancing
Wrought the thing she willed:—
Mobs of us made noble
By her strong desire,
By her white, uplifting,
Royal romance-fire.

Though the tin piano
Snarls its tango rude,
Though the chairs are shaky
And the dramas crude,
Solemn are her motions,
Stately are her wiles,
Filling oafs with wisdom,
Saving souls with smiles;
'Mid the restless actors
She is rich and slow.
She will stand like marble,
She will pause and glow,
Though the film is twitching,
Keep a peaceful reign,
Ruler of her passion,
Ruler of our pain!

Sunshine

FOR A VERY LITTLE GIRL, NOT A YEAR OLD.
CATHARINE FRAZEE WAKEFIELD.

The sun gives not directly
    The coal, the diamond crown;
Not in a special basket
    Are these from Heaven let down.

The sun gives not directly
    The plough, man's iron friend;
Not by a path or stairway
    Do tools from Heaven descend.

Yet sunshine fashions all things
    That cut or burn or fly;
And corn that seems upon the earth
    Is made in the hot sky.

The gravel of the roadbed,
    The metal of the gun,
The engine of the airship
    Trace somehow from the sun.

And so your soul, my lady—
    (Mere sunshine, nothing more)—
Prepares me the contraptions
    I work with or adore.

Within me cornfields rustle,
    Niagaras roar their way,
Vast thunderstorms and rainbows
    Are in my thought to-day.

Ten thousand anvils sound there
    By forges flaming white,
And many books I read there,
    And many books I write;

And freedom's bells are ringing,
    And bird-choirs chant and fly—
The whole world works in me to-day
    And all the shining sky,

Because of one small lady
  Whose smile is my chief sun.
She gives not any gift to me
  Yet all gifts, giving one. . . .
                              Amen.

An Apology for the Bottle Volcanic

Sometimes I dip my pen and find the bottle full of fire,
The salamanders flying forth I cannot but admire.
It's Etna, or Vesuvius, if those big things were small,
And then 'tis but itself again, and does not smoke at all.
And so my blood grows cold. I say, "The bottle held but ink,
And, if you thought it otherwise, the worser for your think."
And then, just as I throw my scribbled paper on the floor,
The bottle says, "Fe, fi, fo, fum," and steams and shouts
      some more.
O sad deceiving ink, as bad as liquor in its way—
All demons of a bottle size have pranced from you to-day,
And seized my pen for hobby-horse as witches ride a broom,
And left a trail of brimstone words, and blots and gobs of gloom.
And yet when I am extra good and say my prayers at night,
And mind my ma, and do the chores, and speak to folks polite,
My bottle spreads a rainbow-mist, and from the vapor fine
Ten thousand troops from fairyland come riding in a line.
I've seen them on their chargers race around my study chair,
They opened wide the window and rode forth upon the air.
The army widened as it went, and into myriads grew,
O how the lances shimmered, how the silvery trumpets blew!

When Gassy Thompson Struck It Rich

He paid a Swede twelve bits an hour
Just to invent a fancy style
To spread the celebration paint
So it would show at least a mile.

Some things they did I will not tell.
They're not quite proper for a rhyme.
But I WILL say Yim Yonson Swede
Did sure invent a sunflower time.

One thing they did that I can tell
And not offend the ladies here:—
They took a goat to Simp's Saloon
And made it take a bath in beer.

That ENTERprise took MANagement.
They broke a wash-tub in the fray.
But mister goat was bathed all right
And bar-keep Simp was, too, they say.

They wore girls' pink straw hats to church
And clucked like hens. They surely did.
They bought two HOtel frying pans
And in them down the mountain slid.

They went to Denver in good clothes,
And kept Burt's grill-room wide awake,
And cut about like jumping-jacks,
And ordered seven-dollar steak.

They had the waiters whirling round
Just sweeping up the smear and smash.
They tried to buy the State-house flag.
They showed the Janitor the cash.

And old Dan Tucker on a toot,
Or John Paul Jones before the breeze,
Or Indians eating fat fried dog,
Were not as happy babes as these.

One morn, in hills near Cripple-creek
With cheerful swears the two awoke.
The Swede had twenty cents, all right.
But Gassy Thompson was clean broke.

SECOND SECTION: RHYMES FOR GLORIANA

The Doll upon the Topmost Bough

This doll upon the topmost bough,
This playmate-gift, in Christmas dress,
Was taken down and brought to me
One sleety night most comfortless.

Her hair was gold, her dolly-sash
Was gray brocade, most good to see.
The dear toy laughed, and I forgot
The ill the new year promised me.

On Suddenly Receiving a Curl Long Refused

Oh, saucy gold circle of fairyland silk—
Impudent, intimate, delicate treasure:
A noose for my heart and a ring for my finger:—
Here in my study you sing me a measure.

Whimsy and song in my little gray study!
Words out of wonderland, praising her fineness,
Touched with her pulsating, delicate laughter,
Saying, "The girl is all daring and kindness!"

Saying, "Her soul is all feminine gameness,
Trusting her insights, ardent for living;
She would be weeping with me and be laughing,
A thoroughbred, joyous receiving and giving!"

On Receiving One of Gloriana's Letters

Your pen needs but a ruffle
To be Pavlova whirling.
It surely is a scalawag
A-scamping down the page.

A pretty little May-wind
The morning buds uncurling.
And then the white sweet Russian,
The dancer of the age.

Your pen's the Queen of Sheba,
Such serious questions bringing,
That merry rascal Solomon
Would show a sober face:—
And then again Pavlova
To set our spirits singing,
The snowy-swan bacchante
All glamour, glee and grace.

In Praise of Gloriana's Remarkable Golden Hair

The gleaming head of one fine friend
Is bent above my little song,
So through the treasure-pits of Heaven
In fancy's shoes, I march along.

I wander, seek and peer and ponder
In Splendor's last ensnaring lair—
'Mid burnished harps and burnished crowns
Where noble chariots gleam and flare:

Amid the spirit-coins and gems,
The plates and cups and helms of fire—
The gorgeous-treasure-pits of Heaven—
Where angel-misers slake desire!

O endless treasure-pits of gold
Where silly angel-men make mirth—
I think that I am there this hour,
Though walking in the ways of earth!

TWENTY POEMS IN WHICH THE MOON IS THE PRINCIPAL FIGURE OF SPEECH

Once More—To Gloriana

Girl with the burning golden eyes,
And red-bird song, and snowy throat:
I bring you gold and silver moons
And diamond stars, and mists that float.
I bring you moons and snowy clouds,
I bring you prairie skies to-night
To feebly praise your golden eyes
And red-bird song, and throat so white.

First Section: Moon Poems for the Children

Euclid

Old Euclid drew a circle
On a sand-beach long ago.
He bounded and enclosed it
With angles thus and so.
His set of solemn greybeards
Nodded and argued much
Of arc and of circumference,
Diameter and such.
A silent child stood by them
From morning until noon
Because they drew such charming
Round pictures of the moon.

The Haughty Snail-King

(*What Uncle William Told the Children*)

Twelve snails went walking after night.
They'd creep an inch or so,
Then stop and bug their eyes
And blow.
Some folks . . . are . . . deadly . . . slow.

Twelve snails went walking yestereve,
Led by their fat old king.
They were so dull their princeling had
No sceptre, robe or ring—
Only a paper cap to wear
When nightly journeying.

This king-snail said: "I feel a thought
Within. . . . It blossoms soon. . . .
O little courtiers of mine, . . .
I crave a pretty boon. . . .
Oh, yes . . . (High thoughts with effort come
And well-bred snails are ALMOST dumb.)
"I wish I had a yellow crown
As glistering . . . as . . . the moon."

What the Rattlesnake Said

The moon's a little prairie-dog.
He shivers through the night.
He sits upon his hill and cries
For fear that *I* will bite.

The sun's a broncho. He's afraid
Like every other thing,
And trembles, morning, noon and night,
Lest *I* should spring, and sting.

The Moon's the North Wind's Cooky

(*What the Little Girl Said*)

The Moon's the North Wind's cooky.
He bites it, day by day,
Until there's but a rim of scraps
That crumble all away.

The South Wind is a baker.
He kneads clouds in his den,
And bakes a crisp new moon *that . . . greedy
North . . . Wind . . . eats . . . again!*

Drying Their Wings

(What the Carpenter Said)

The moon's a cottage with a door.
Some folks can see it plain.
Look, you may catch a glint of light,
A sparkle through the pane,
Showing the place is brighter still
Within, though bright without.
There, at a cosy open fire
Strange babes are grouped about.
The children of the wind and tide—
The urchins of the sky,
Drying their wings from storms and things
So they again can fly.

What the Gray-Winged Fairy Said

The moon's a gong, hung in the wild,
Whose song the fays hold dear.
Of course you do not hear it, child.
It takes a FAIRY ear.
The full moon is a splendid gong
That beats as night grows still.
It sounds above the evening song
Of dove or whippoorwill.

Yet Gentle Will the Griffin Be

(What Grandpa Told the Children)

The moon? It is a griffin's egg,
Hatching to-morrow night.
And how the little boys will watch
With shouting and delight
To see him break the shell and stretch
And creep across the sky.

The boys will laugh. The little girls,
I fear, may hide and cry.
Yet gentle will the griffin be,
Most decorous and fat,
And walk up to the milky way
And lap it like a cat.

SECOND SECTION: THE MOON IS A MIRROR

Prologue. A Sense of Humor

No man should stand before the moon
To make sweet song thereon,
With dandified importance,
His sense of humor gone.

Nay, let us don the motley cap,
The jester's chastened mien,
If we would woo that looking-glass
And see what should be seen.

O mirror on fair Heaven's wall,
We find there what we bring.
So, let us smile in honest part
And deck our souls and sing.

Yea, by the chastened jest alone
Will ghosts and terrors pass,
And fays, or suchlike friendly things,
Throw kisses through the glass.

On the Garden-Wall

Oh, once I walked a garden
In dreams. 'Twas yellow grass.
And many orange-trees grew there
In sand as white as glass.
The curving, wide wall-border
Was marble, like the snow.

I walked that wall a fairy-prince
And, pacing quaint and slow,
Beside me were my pages,
Two giant, friendly birds.
Half-swan they were, half peacock.
They spake in courtier-words.
Their inner wings a chariot,
Their outer wings for flight,
They lifted me from dreamland.
We bade those trees good-night.
Swiftly above the stars we rode.
I looked below me soon.
The white-walled garden I had ruled
Was one lone flower—the moon.

Written for a Musician

Hungry for music with a desperate hunger
I prowled abroad, I threaded through the town;
The evening crowd was clamoring and drinking,
Vulgar and pitiful—my heart bowed down—
Till I remembered duller hours made noble
By strangers clad in some surprising grace.
Wait, wait, my soul, your music comes ere midnight
Appearing in some unexpected place
With quivering lips, and gleaming, moonlit face.

The Moon Is a Painter

He coveted her portrait.
He toiled as she grew gay.
She loved to see him labor
In that devoted way.

And in the end it pleased her,
But bowed him more with care.
Her rose-smile showed so plainly,
Her soul-smile was not there.

That night he groped without a lamp
To find a cloak, a book,
And on the vexing portrait
By moonrise chanced to look.

The color-scheme was out of key,
The maiden rose-smile faint,
But through the blessed darkness
She gleamed, his friendly saint.

The comrade, white, immortal,
His bride, and more than bride—
The citizen, the sage of mind,
For whom he lived and died.

The Encyclopaedia

"If I could set the moon upon
This table," said my friend,
"Among the standard poets
And brochures without end,
And noble prints of old Japan,
How empty they would seem,
By that encyclopaedia
Of whim and glittering dream."

What the Miner in the Desert Said

The moon's a brass-hooped water-keg,
A wondrous water-feast.
If I could climb the ridge and drink
And give drink to my beast;
If I could drain that keg, the flies
Would not be biting so,
My burning feet be spry again,
My mule no longer slow.
And I could rise and dig for ore,
And reach my fatherland,
And not be food for ants and hawks
And perish in the sand.

What the Coal-Heaver Said

The moon's an open furnace door
Where all can see the blast,
We shovel in our blackest griefs,
Upon that grate are cast
Our aching burdens, loves and fears
And underneath them wait
Paper and tar and pitch and pine
Called strife and blood and hate.

Out of it all there comes a flame,
A splendid widening light.
Sorrow is turned to mystery
And Death into delight.

What the Moon Saw

Two statesmen met by moonlight.
Their ease was partly feigned.
They glanced about the prairie.
Their faces were constrained.
In various ways aforetime
They had misled the state,
Yet did it so politely
Their henchmen thought them great.
They sat beneath a hedge and spake
No word, but had a smoke.
A satchel passed from hand to hand.
Next day, the deadlock broke.

What Semiramis Said

The moon's a steaming chalice
    Of honey and venom-wine.
A little of it sipped by night
    Makes the long hours divine.
But oh, my reckless lovers,
    They drain the cup and wail,

Die at my feet with shaking limbs
    And tender lips all pale.
Above them in the sky it bends
    Empty and gray and dread.
To-morrow night 'tis full again,
    Golden, and foaming red.

What the Ghost of the Gambler Said

Where now the huts are empty,
Where never a camp-fire glows,
In an abandoned cañon,
A Gambler's Ghost arose.
He muttered there, "The moon's a sack
Of dust." His voice rose thin:
"I wish I knew the miner-man.
I'd play, and play to win.
In every game in Cripple-creek
Of old, when stakes were high,
I held my own. Now I would play
For that sack in the sky.
The sport would not be ended there.
'Twould rather be begun.
I'd bet my moon against his stars,
And gamble for the sun."

The Spice-Tree

This is the song
The spice-tree sings:
"Hunger and fire,
Hunger and fire,
Sky-born Beauty—
Spice of desire,"
Under the spice-tree
Watch and wait,
Burning maidens
And lads that mate.

The spice-tree spreads
And its boughs come down
Shadowing village and farm and town.
And none can see
But the pure of heart
The great green leaves
And the boughs descending,
And hear the song that is never ending.

The deep roots whisper,
The branches say:—
"Love to-morrow,
And love to-day,
And till Heaven's day,
And till Heaven's day."

The moon is a bird's nest in its branches,
The moon is hung in its topmost spaces.
And there, to-night, two doves play house
While lovers watch with uplifted faces.
Two doves go home
To their nest, the moon.
It is woven of twigs of broken light,
With threads of scarlet and threads of gray
And a lining of down for silk delight.
To their Eden, the moon, fly home our doves,
Up through the boughs of the great spice-tree;—
And one is the kiss I took from you,
And one is the kiss you gave to me.

The Scissors-Grinder

(What the Tramp Said)

The old man had his box and wheel
For grinding knives and shears.
No doubt his bell in village streets
Was joy to children's ears.
And I bethought me of my youth
When such men came around,
And times I asked them in, quite sure
The scissors should be ground.

The old man turned and spoke to me,
His face at last in view.
And then I thought those curious eyes
Were eyes that once I knew.

"The moon is but an emery-wheel
To whet the sword of God,"
He said. "And here beside my fire
I stretch upon the sod
Each night, and dream, and watch the stars
And watch the ghost-clouds go.
And see that sword of God in Heaven
A-waving to and fro.
I see that sword each century, friend.
It means the world-war comes
With all its bloody, wicked chiefs
And hate-inflaming drums.
Men talk of peace, but I have seen
That emery-wheel turn round.
The voice of Abel cries again
To God from out the ground.
The ditches must flow red, the plague
Go stark and screaming by
Each time that sword of God takes edge
Within the midnight sky.
And those that scorned their brothers here
And sowed a wind of shame
Will reap the whirlwind as of old
And face relentless flame."

And thus the scissors-grinder spoke,
His face at last in view.
And there beside the railroad bridge
I saw the wandering Jew.

My Lady in Her White Silk Shawl

My lady in her white silk shawl
    Is like a lily dim,
Within the twilight of the room
    Enthroned and kind and prim.

My lady! Pale gold is her hair.
  Until she smiles her face
Is pale with far Hellenic moods,
  With thoughts that find no place

In our harsh village of the West
  Wherein she lives of late,
She's distant as far-hidden stars,
  And cold—(almost!)—as fate.

But when she smiles she's here again
  Rosy with comrade-cheer,
A Puritan Bacchante made
  To laugh around the year.

The merry gentle moon herself,
  Heart-stirring too, like her,
Wakening wild and innocent love
  In every worshipper.

Aladdin and the Jinn

"Bring me soft song," said Aladdin.
"This tailor-shop sings not at all.
Chant me a word of the twilight,
Of roses that mourn in the fall.
Bring me a song like hashish
That will comfort the stale and the sad,
For I would be mending my spirit,
Forgetting these days that are bad,
Forgetting companions too shallow,
Their quarrels and arguments thin,
Forgetting the shouting Muezzin:"—
"I AM YOUR SLAVE," said the Jinn.

"Bring me old wines," said Aladdin.
"I have been a starved pauper too long.
Serve them in vessels of jade and of shell,
Serve them with fruit and with song:—
Wines of pre-Adamite Sultans
Digged from beneath the black seas:—
New-gathered dew from the heavens

Dripped down from Heaven's sweet trees,
Cups from the angels' pale tables
That will make me both handsome and wise,
For I have beheld her, the princess,
Firelight and starlight her eyes.
Pauper I am, I would woo her.
And—let me drink wine, to begin,
Though the Koran expressly forbids it."
"I AM YOUR SLAVE," said the Jinn.

"Plan me a dome," said Aladdin,
"That is drawn like the dawn of the MOON,
When the sphere seems to rest on the mountains,
Half-hidden, yet full-risen soon."
"Build me a dome," said Aladdin,
"That shall cause all young lovers to sigh,
The fullness of life and of beauty,
Peace beyond peace to the eye—
A palace of foam and of opal,
Pure moonlight without and within,
Where I may enthrone my sweet lady."
"I AM YOUR SLAVE," said the Jinn.

The Strength of the Lonely

(*What the Mendicant Said*)

The moon's a monk, unmated,
Who walks his cell, the sky.
His strength is that of heaven-vowed men
Who all life's flames defy.

They turn to stars or shadows,
They go like snow or dew—
Leaving behind no sorrow—
Only the arching blue.

WAR. SEPTEMBER 1, 1914
INTENDED TO BE READ ALOUD

Abraham Lincoln Walks at Midnight

(In Springfield, Illinois)

It is portentous, and a thing of state
That here at midnight, in our little town
A mourning figure walks, and will not rest,
Near the old court-house pacing up and down,

Or by his homestead, or in shadowed yards
He lingers where his children used to play,
Or through the market, on the well-worn stones
He stalks until the dawn-stars burn away.

A bronzed, lank man! His suit of ancient black,
A famous high top-hat and plain worn shawl
Make him the quaint great figure that men love,
The prairie-lawyer, master of us all.

He cannot sleep upon his hillside now.
He is among us:—as in times before!
And we who toss and lie awake for long
Breathe deep, and start, to see him pass the door.

His head is bowed. He thinks on men and kings.
Yea, when the sick world cries, how can he sleep?
Too many peasants fight, they know not why,
Too many homesteads in black terror weep.

The sins of all the war-lords burn his heart.
He sees the dreadnaughts scouring every main.
He carries on his shawl-wrapped shoulders now
The bitterness, the folly and the pain.

He cannot rest until a spirit-dawn
Shall come;—the shining hope of Europe free:
The league of sober folk, the Workers' Earth,
Bringing long peace to Cornland, Alp and Sea.

It breaks his heart that kings must murder still,
That all his hours of travail here for men
Seem yet in vain. And who will bring white peace
That he may sleep upon his hill again?

A Curse for Kings

A curse upon each king who leads his state,
No matter what his plea, to this foul game,
And may it end his wicked dynasty,
And may he die in exile and black shame.

If there is vengeance in the Heaven of Heavens,
What punishment could Heaven devise for these
Who fill the rivers of the world with dead,
And turn their murderers loose on all the seas!

Put back the clock of time a thousand years,
And make our Europe, once the world's proud Queen,
A shrieking strumpet, furious fratricide,
Eater of entrails, wallowing obscene

In pits where millions foam and rave and bark,
Mad dogs and idiots, thrice drunk with strife;
While Science towers above;—a witch, red-winged:
Science we looked to for the light of life.

Curse me the men who make and sell iron ships,
Who walk the floor in thought, that they may find
Each powder prompt, each steel with fearful edge,
Each deadliest device against mankind.

Curse me the sleek lords with their plumes and spurs,
May Heaven give their land to peasant spades,
Give them the brand of Cain, for their pride's sake,
And felon's stripes for medals and for braids.

Curse me the fiddling, twiddling diplomats,
Haggling here, plotting and hatching there,
Who make the kind world but their game of cards,
Till millions die at turning of a hair.

What punishment will Heaven devise for these
Who win by others' sweat and hardihood,
Who make men into stinking vultures' meat,
Saying to evil still "Be thou my good"?

Ah, he who starts a million souls toward death
Should burn in utmost hell a million years!
—Mothers of men go on the destined wrack
To give them life, with anguish and with tears:—

Are all those childbed sorrows sneered away?
Yea, fools laugh at the humble christenings,
And cradle-joys are mocked of the fat lords:
These mothers' sons made dead men for the Kings!

All in the name of this or that grim flag,
No angel-flags in all the rag-array—
Banners the demons love, and all Hell sings
And plays wild harps. Those flags march forth to-day!

Who Knows?

They say one king is mad. Perhaps. Who knows?
They say one king is doddering and grey.
They say one king is slack and sick of mind,
A puppet for hid strings that twitch and play.

Is Europe then to be their sprawling-place?
Their mad-house, till it turns the wide world's bane?
Their place of maudlin, slavering conference
Till every far-off farmstead goes insane?

To Buddha

Awake again in Asia, Lord of Peace,
Awake and preach, for her far swordsmen rise.
And would they sheathe the sword before you, friend,
Or scorn your way, while looking in your eyes?

Good comrade and philosopher and prince,
Thoughtful and thoroughbred and strong and kind,
Dare they to move against your pride benign,
Lord of the Law, high chieftain of the mind?

*　　　*　　　*　　　*　　　*

But what can Europe say, when in your name
The throats are cut, the lotus-ponds turn red?
And what can Europe say, when with a laugh
Old Asia heaps her hecatombs of dead?

The Unpardonable Sin

This is the sin against the Holy Ghost:—
To speak of bloody power as right divine,
And call on God to guard each vile chiefs house,
And for such chiefs, turn men to wolves and swine:—

To go forth killing in White Mercy's name,
Making the trenches stink with spattered brains,
Tearing the nerves and arteries apart,
Sowing with flesh the unreaped golden plains.

In any Church's name, to sack fair towns,
And turn each home into a screaming sty,
To make the little children fugitive,
And have their mothers for a quick death cry,—

This is the sin against the Holy Ghost:
This is the sin no purging can atone:—
To send forth rapine in the name of Christ:—
To set the face, and make the heart a stone.

Above the Battle's Front

St. Francis, Buddha, Tolstoi, and St. John—
Friends, if you four, as pilgrims, hand in hand,
Returned, the hate of earth once more to dare,
And walked upon the water and the land,

If you, with words celestial, stopped these kings
For sober conclave, ere their battle great,
Would they for one deep instant then discern
Their crime, their heart-rot, and their fiend's estate?

If you should float above the battle's front,
Pillars of cloud, of fire that does not slay,
Bearing a fifth within your regal train,
The Son of David in his strange array—

If, in his majesty, he towered toward Heaven,
Would they have hearts to see or understand?
. . . Nay, for he hovers there to-night we know,
Thorn-crowned above the water and the land.

Epilogue

Under the Blessing of Your Psyche Wings

Though I have found you like a snow-drop pale,
On sunny days have found you weak and still,
Though I have often held your girlish head
Drooped on my shoulder, faint from little ill:—

Under the blessing of your Psyche-wings
I hide to-night like one small broken bird,
So soothed I half-forget the world gone mad:—
And all the winds of war are now unheard.

My heaven-doubting pennons feel your hands
With touch most delicate so circling round,
That for an hour I dream that God is good.
And in your shadow, Mercy's ways abound.

I thought myself the guard of your frail state,
And yet I come to-night a helpless guest,
Hiding beneath your giant Psyche-wings,
Against the pallor of your wondrous breast.

ALPHABETICAL LIST OF TITLES